Isle Full of Noises

Kevin Densley

Acknowledgements

Poems in this book previously appeared, sometimes in slightly different form, in *Quadrant*, *micropress oz* and *The Footy Almanac*.

A big thank you to Terry Matassoni for the front and back cover art.

Front cover image: *Man, Thylacine, Devil, Fire* (2025),
by Terry Matassoni, oil on linen, 41cm by 61cm

Inside back cover image: *Portrait of Kevin Densley* (2025),
by Terry Matassoni, oil on linen, 36cm by 46cm

Isle Full of Noises
Copyright©2026 Kevin Densley
Print ISBN: 978-1-76109-734-8
ebook ISBN: 978-1-76109-735-5

First published 2026 by
GINNINDERRA PRESS
PO Box 2 Bentleigh 3204
ginninderrapress.com.au

(Caliban speaks to Stephano and Trinculo.)

'Be not afeard; the isle is full of noises,
Sounds and sweet airs, that give delight, and hurt not.
Sometimes a thousand twangling instruments
Will hum about mine ears; and sometime voices,
That, if I then had waked after long sleep,
Will make me sleep again: and then, in dreaming,
The clouds methought would open, and show riches
Ready to drop upon me; that, when I waked,
I cried to dream again.'

> Shakespeare, *The Tempest,* Act III, Scene II

Contents

Music Heard in Rural France in the Sixteenth Century	6
Big Bopper Junior Meets His Late Father	7
Another Song for Severed Head	9
The Arnolfini Divorce: A Portrait	10
Neurotic Worry	12
Birds	13
Albert Jacka, Australia's First VC of The Great War	14
Chad Morgan, the Sheik of Scrubby Creek, Rueful and Reflective after Getting Clobbered from Behind by a Piece of Two-Be-Four while Having a Piss in the Back Paddock of an Outback Pub During an Interval in his Country-and-Western Show	15
A Pilgrimage to San Isidro	16
Fighting Planes of World War Two	17
E(a)rnest	18
Eurotrash	19
Devolution	20
The Fish of Geelong	21
Forget the Metaphor	24
Essay in Loneliness	25
Ann Arbor, Michigan	26
Good Old Unca	27
Goya's *El Pelele (The Straw Manikin)*	29
Happy Families	30
Google Earth	31
Asinine	33
In Praise of Ingres' *La Grande Odalisque*	34
I am Jesus Christ	35
Jubilee Lake, Daylesford	36
Italianesque	37

Larkin's Last Words	38
Life is Such	39
Memento Mori	41
Mitchell Library, Sydney, 1997	42
All Dead Now	43
'Ned Kelly Photograph', circa 1875	44
On Kandinski's *Dreamy Improvisation* (1913)	46
Penthesilea	47
Observing the Artist Observing	48
The Poet Who Got the Grant Instead of You	49
'Pilate's Wife's Dream' Revisited	50
Rampantly Bad Poets' Society	51
Sequence of Dreams	53
Picture at an Exhibition: *'Solo Man' (homo softdrinkus)* c. 1975, Australia	54
Brief Biographical Sketch of Titian	55
This/That?	56
Chaos Theory	57
Variations on Some Lines from Plath's 'Lorelei'	58
The Geelong College Gates, Geelong, Victoria	59
What I Remember About My Paternal Grandfather	60
When Colonel Sanders Met Colonel Tom Parker	61
Writer's Lament	62
All Hallows' Eve	63
Not Quite Yorick	64
When the Dead Return	65
Semaphore, Adelaide	66
To Die	68

Music Heard in Rural France in the Sixteenth Century

Sackbuts reverberate across the fields,
sticks *rat-tat-tat* against pigskin drums,
bagpipes blare,
recorders trill like finches
and strings played with rough-hewn bows
squeak and grind
as they wind in and out of the other sounds.
Then standard-bearers
on their horses
appear over the rise.

Big Bopper Junior Meets His Late Father

J. P. Richardson Junior
successfully obtained
a forensic study
of his father's corpse
in 2007,
to confirm or refute the theory
that Bopper Senior initially survived
the plane crash in an icy cornfield
in Clear Lake, Iowa,
forty eight years earlier,
a catastrophe that killed
all on board –
Buddy Holly, Richie Valens
and Peterson the pilot,
as well as himself.
The theory of initial survival
arose from finding Bopper Senior's body
forty feet from the others.
Did Senior not die immediately
and crawled for help
before succumbing to injuries?
That was the question.

J. P. Junior and his fellow
attendees at the coffin's opening,
saw a corpse in remarkably good condition.

(A waterproof steel casket did its work.)
The coiffed crewcut was intact
and the figure,
dressed in a plain black suit
and blue-and-grey striped tie,
at odds with its flamboyant subject,
recognisably that of the Bopper,
in spite of a slightly shrunken head,
bloated hands and feet
and bluish skin.
(Oh, and there was the smell,
the terrible smell.)

The examining doctor concluded,
on the basis of x-ray analysis,
that virtually every bone
in the body had been broken
and the original Bopper
died on impact,
his body flung
away from the other three.
Aside from incidental comments
and his removal of a lock
of the ol' rocker's hair,
Bopper Junior declared,
concerning the father he never knew,
being born three months
after Senior's death:
'Dad looked in pretty good shape, really.'

Another Song for Severed Head

Well. Here's the *shtick*.
Write an opera libretto or play.
Get the hero (or villain,
it doesn't matter)
decapitated by sword, guillotined,
headless in some way.
Then write a lyric to be sung
by the severed head.
Of course, like everything, it's been done.
But why not do it again?
Rhetorically, it's intriguing.
The audience will think you're clever.
Definitely worth a try.

The Arnolfini Divorce: A Portrait
'long after' the fifteenth century painting by Jan van Eyck

The two young married couples
came here
from the old country,
with no more than a suitcase
and the clothes they stood up in.
They lived in rented flats, had kids,
worked long hours to give their children
a better life,
saved their money, went without,
and sent their offspring to private Catholic schools.
The oldest son and daughter
of each family married
then moved to a solid brick, middle-class house
in the midst of suburbia.
In less than a year,
they fell apart
– he went to nightclubs,
had an affair with a girl in the office.
His wife was howling and pregnant
when she booted him out the door.
The divorce did not go smoothly.
An ugly fight ensued
over assets, child
and greatly loved
shaggy, brown-haired terrier.

But Mr. and Mrs. Arnolfini,
eventually,
wandered off to new lives,
with new partners,
still in the same part of town.

Neurotic Worry

The empty glass
pickle jar

shattered on the
unforgiving

concrete outside
my back door.

I swept it up with the utmost care.

But in ten years' time
a spiny shard

could disappear
with terrible pain

into someone's heel.

And it would be my fault.

Birds

are fallen angels
– beaky,
beady-eyed
winged, feathered
devils.

Albert Jacka, Australia's First VC of The Great War

(Courtney's Post, Gallipoli, May 19-20, 1915)

Wielding a bolt action
Enfield 303,
bayonet attached,
in a feat of brilliant athleticism
as much as bravery,
Lance-Corporal Jacka leaps into a trench,
shoots dead five Turks,
bayonets two more.
The remainder 'think it best to leave'.
His platoon commander,
Crabbe, finds him
after the affray
leaning against the parados,
having held this part of the trench – by himself –
for more than a quarter hour,
face flushed, unlit cigarette
dangling from his lips:
'I managed to get the beggars, sir.'

Chad Morgan, the Sheik of Scrubby Creek, Rueful and Reflective after Getting Clobbered from Behind by a Piece of Two-Be-Four while Having a Piss in the Back Paddock of an Outback Pub During an Interval in his Country-and-Western Show

Strewth,
a bloke needs eyes
in the back of his fucken head
when takin a leak
at a joint like this.
Was prob'ly that bloke before,
the one near the river this arvo,
who I aimed at with me 303.
Only meant to scare the bugger.

A Pilgrimage to San Isidro

after a painting by Goya

Parched faces –
in a scorched landscape –
Everything seems burnt –

The corners of the canvas curl,
blacken and send up plumes of smoke.

Fighting Planes of World War Two

As a kid, it seemed a good idea,
exciting, fun
– when I looked at the cover of the box
in the department store
a Spitfire, Lancaster, Zero appeared
in all its vivid glory.
Why not try to build one?

But the parts were tiny, plastic, fiddly,
the glue impossibly sticky
and would congeal around the cap
almost as soon as I'd opened the tube.
As for the delicate brushes,
those tiny paint tins,
to decorate the fuselage...

I never had the patience
to properly complete
one of these stupid planes.
Inevitably, my efforts
resulted in a load of crap.

E(a)rnest

Hemingway drowned
in the wake
of his imitators.

He struggled to the surface
once or twice
before the tsunami overwhelmed.

Eurotrash

Versace's gold Medusa.
Post-punk fashion in Paris.
Slender high-breasted Über-babes
strolling in Berlin,
androgynous, chrome-skinned,
impossibly blonde,
depressingly robotic
new millennium girls.

Devolution

Debating the master.
Master-debating.
Master-baiting.

Having a wank.

The Fish of Geelong

When I was a kid in Geelong,
I fished.

Below are the fish of Geelong I knew.
All in my head by the age of twelve.

Freshwater fish,
mainly from the Barwon River:
brown trout,
carp,
eels,
rainbow trout
and redfin.

Saltwater fish,
mainly from Corio Bay
– many could be caught by line
from Cunningham Pier
in the middle of the city:
banjo shark,
barracuda,
bream,
bronze whaler shark,
butterfish,
flathead,
flounder,

garfish,
gummy shark,
John Dory,
leatherjacket (cut out the prickle on its back
– this is not to be eaten),
school shark,
sea horses (I caught one in a net – illegal),
snapper,
stingray,
toadfish (poisonous),
trevally,
whiting
and wobbegong.

Such are
– perhaps, in some cases, were
the fish of Geelong,
at least, ones known to me.

How many did I catch? Not many.
Was I a good fisherman? No.
I was too impatient, and was repulsed

by the hack of the knife,
the blood,
the death.

I went fishing, simply,

because water was near
and for the experience;
in some ways, I knew
my subject well.

....

(Note: some water creatures are not fish,
of course
– Geelong had plenty of these:
black mussels,
crabs,
cuttlefish,
limpets,
octopus [poisonous and otherwise],
shrimp,
squid,
yabbies...)

Forget the Metaphor

One Aesop's fable
full of shit
is 'The Tortoise and the Hare':

a hare,
if it's a real hare,
will whip a tortoise's arse
every time.

Essay in Loneliness

You're teaching at the regional campus
of a small university;
single, new to all your colleagues.
They're friendly enough, but never
invite you 'round for tea.
You stay at cheap motels, pubs,
drink too much in the evening.
(There's nothing else to do.)
Listen to the racing station
as you go to sleep.
In time, the calf
of your right leg
feels very sore,
as if the muscle
has torn from the bone.
You're diagnosed
with an aneurysm
behind your right knee.
You survive the big operation
to remove the obstruction.
Then you get to now.
You have a similar job,
in another similar place.

Ann Arbor, Michigan

No – I've got nothing really,
not a word
about the place itself,
except that Ann Arbor has to be
the most beautiful name for a city
I've ever heard.

Good Old Unca

My mate Tom had an uncle
he disparagingly nicknamed 'Unca'.
For three years Unca freeloaded
at Tom's family home
where all he did was guzzle sherry
and listen to the races.
Unca annoyed the shit out of Tom
because of his slackarse ways.
Before long, Tom found it hard
to even grunt at the bloke.
He'd have whooped and danced with joy
if he heard that Unca was leaving.
How it ended, I didn't know
till I talked to Tom later.
Attempting humour, I said,
'Well, at least he didn't knife anyone.'
Tom raised an eyebrow,
'Actually, he tried.' Then related the tale
of how tottering, rheumy old Unca
pulled a blade on Mick (Tom's dad)
at the breakfast table.
'Come on, M-Mick. I'll h-have ya!'
stuttered the tiny, pathetic fool.
'Pack up your gear and bugger off!' roared Mick,
dismissing the threat with the wave of his hand.

Unca cowered.
He left within the hour,
disappearing, somewhere down the road,
into a dark brown bottle.

Goya's *El Pelele (The Straw Manikin)*

Here we go!
Up, now!
the pretty smiling ladies cry
as they toss me off the blanket
high into the air.
I feel all strange,
rubbery,
floppy-limbed and brainless.
The sky is at a weird angle.
Everyone's having fun but me.

Happy Families

Mum won't talk to Aunt Thelma
and son won't talk to dad (except mutter).
The sisters talk to each other (that's good)
but one won't speak to brother
and brother definitely won't speak to her.
Of course, way back, mum's mother
had a falling out with her sister,
while her mother and father's parents
never got on at all.
Other than that, what can I say?

Everything's bliss.

Google Earth

(a true story)

Typical scene
in an Australian
industrial town:
an outer suburb
bakes in red dust,
beneath a boiling sun.
Google Earth visits the street,
capturing it in images.
The woman,
laughing to herself,
thinks why not?
Stands in front of her house,
on the footpath,
whips her T-shirt
over her head.
No bra,
revealing basketball boobs,
orbs that make busty celebs
the world over
look like women
with 'insufficient flying buttresses',
which is how a theatre critic described
the top half of Dame Diana Rigg
when she appeared nude on stage.

But back to the tale...
The husband of Mrs Topless
in the Australian town
is supportive in the image
Google Earth makes,
standing, to one side, behind her
on their scraggly front lawn,
dragging on a smoke,
as his wife shares her tits with half the world,
while a kid (presumably her son)
sits on their small front porch
looking the other way,
apparently bored,
doesn't care at all,
about Mum's gleeful reveal
of her mountainous mammaries.

Asinine

On Palm Sunday,
Our Lord
rode into town
on a jackass.
Or was it a donkey?

Is there a difference?

In Praise of Ingres' *La Grande Odalisque*

Ah! La Grande Odalisque!
I imagine, on compact disc,
music set to the work of Ingres,
including a solo for violin
with a melody which seems to run
along the long, sensual back
of La Grande Odalisque herself.

The neo-classical elegance
of this wonderful art
reminds us that life
is not just snags and vegetables
for evening meals
and catching early trains to work
on howling winter mornings;
for certain, *La Grande Odalisque*
is that glorious 'something extra'.

I am Jesus Christ

Psychosis, of course,
is partly a cultural thing
– if it wasn't, then we wouldn't see ourselves
as members of the monarchy
or well-known biblical figures.

Jubilee Lake, Daylesford

How deep is Jubilee Lake?
What does the blue darkness conceal?
Will reeds on the bottom
clutch at my limbs
when I dive into its mystery?
Will I flail into oblivion?
Asphyxiate in shadows and murk?

Can I survive my journey
to the bottom of Jubilee Lake
when I go down there?

Italianesque

(to Dante Gabriel Rossetti)

The women in your paintings are
Italianesque.
Your canvases exude
Italianate sensuousness –
the line of jaw, of lips and nose,
the fall of the drapery,
all go to show, though you're English-born,
a touch created by Italy.

Larkin's Last Words

On his deathbed, Philip Larkin
turned to his nurse and said,
'I am going to the inevitable'

– not surprising, being a poet,
that he got out something so fluent.

Life is Such

Last night I dreamt
I shot Ned Kelly
in the back.

He'd surrendered,
was compliant.
I didn't think he'd run.

But then he made a sudden move,
a last-ditch effort
to escape.

Without thinking,
I pulled the trigger
– a groan,

then that tall,
surprisingly slender,
athletic, bearded man

dropped to the ground with a thud.
The chase had been long.
And the law had been on my side.

I was too tired to feel much.
But I wish the bastard hadn't run.
I'd started to like him.

Goodbye, Ned.
So sorry I shot you like a dog.

Memento Mori

Looking into a mirror,
not liking what I see
– there's a skeleton on the other side,
laughing hysterically.

Mitchell Library, Sydney, 1997

Neoclassical architecture's
wonderful,
especially on this hilltop
overlooking these breezy gardens
that roll down to the waterfront
of this ridiculously blue
most beautiful harbour in the world.

All Dead Now

Sylvia Plath on a beach in Nauset
T. S. Eliot answering the phone
in his office at Faber and Faber
Dylan Thomas
drinking Guinness in a Welsh pub
The boy Keats in a stable with his father
Shakespeare arguing with a fellow actor
Chaucer taking a piss in a bush
Gerard Manley Hopkins
strolling in an autumnal park
The aged and blind Milton lying in bed,
as if in state
Ezra Pound on the radio
Dickinson buttoning her collar
Whitman watching the naked boys swimming
Emily Bronte with a bulldog in her lap...

'Ned Kelly Photograph', circa 1875

(In 2002, a photograph was auctioned at Christie's in Melbourne as a previously unknown image of Ned Kelly. The picture was authenticated by a Kelly expert who had done much excellent work concerning Ned – but, in this instance, he was soon proved in error by a university specialist in forensic identification.)

James Bray of Beechworth, Victoria,
personal photographer
to the Kelly gang,
took the picture in question.
At some point in their lives,
each of its members
had his photo taken at Bray's:
Ned in boxing attire, fists raised,
fresh from conquering Wild Wright;
Dan, an insecure teenage boy
in an older brother's too-large clothes;
Joe Byrne, *sans* beard,
dapper and urbane,
the bush larrikin only revealed
by the flared riding pants and spurs;
Steve Hart, the sometime jockey,
beady-eyed and wary.
Even Aaron Sherritt, later shot by Byrne
for betrayal,
had his picture taken by Bray,
ironically the only Kelly

supporter to be photographed
as an official sympathizer,
wearing his hat strap under the nose
'Greta fashion'...
Then there's the picture at issue,
purported to be Ned
in his 'quiet man' sawmilling days,
but it's clearly of some bushy
(bearded, yes,
that's the only similarity)
at least a decade older
– I knew that at first glance.
But the noted Kelly specialist
was convinced the photo was of his man,
so keen was he
for something new about Ned.
Obviously, he couldn't see for looking
– but wishing has never made anything so.

On Kandinski's *Dreamy Improvisation* (1913)

What is this
vivid
colour-splotched
-smeared
-splashed
world
in which these
tropical
fish
are swimming?

Penthesilea

Penthesilea, the Amazon Queen,
impulsive, recklessly brave,
plunged into any battle or scrap.
No wonder her death was untimely.

A feminist martyr who proved,
martially, women equal to men?

Or a violent nutcase?

Observing the Artist Observing

There he goes,
fiddling with it,
yet again,
in public.
He's pointing the hideous thing
in our direction.
'No, no Graeme!' we cry,
hands covering our faces.
'Put the fucking camera away!'

The Poet Who Got the Grant Instead of You

Ah, we laughed
...well, I did,
you didn't,
your expression was deadly serious...
when that poet whose work you hated
got the grant instead of you.
You whose pose
was, typically,
to be above
such tawdry, worldly matters
could hardly bear it
– I could see that –
when that poet got the grant instead of you.
I know you needed the money,
desperately.
You seethed when the poet
whose work you firmly believed
was inherently inferior to yours
got that fucking grant instead of you.
You went on about it for hours.
With each beer, your spleen increased
about that no-talent loser
who got the grant instead of you.
Well, mate, she's still going strong
and writing,
decades later, like you.
In the end, who won, who lost?

Who fucking cares?

'Pilate's Wife's Dream' Revisited

Not the dream itself,
but the poem about the dream,
lead-off poem in a slender green
cloth-bound edition of *Poems:
by Currer, Ellis and Acton Bell*,
a self-published volume
the public ignored.
But Currer Bell's poem
launched the print lives
of those three Romantic sisters;
it began a legend, this work
that went behind the scenes
of God's Son's crucifixion.

Rampantly Bad Poets' Society

They sit around the lounge room
at their monthly meetings
reading the tripe they write.

One old man gets misty-eyed
reciting his bush ballad
– one hundred years out of date, mind –

about a faithful dog that died
leaving his tearful master,
a crusty, weatherworn, droving type,

bereft of his only worldly companion.
He deserved to have
his sheaf of papers

shoved up his arse and rotated.
Another reader
at this deplorable gathering,

a senior lecturer in English,
used the word 'deconstruction'
fifteen times in a thirty line poem

– he should have known
the word
is taboo

when it comes
to writing
poetry.

The final reader
at this lamentable
conspiracy of profane souls

did the bloke-in-the-wheat-town-gum-tree-shtick,
where the noble farm labourer
read Paradise Lost every evening

in his bungalow
by torchlight,
freight trains rumbling by in the background.

This 'poet' would not have agreed
with the grey-bearded wonder, Father Marx,
about the 'idiocy of rural life'.

...I left the monthly meeting
of The Rampantly Bad Poets' Society
determined to write about them

in tercets,
with no rhymes
whatsoever.

Sequence of Dreams

I've dreamt I interviewed *The Beatles*
on a late-night TV variety show,
played Test Cricket for Oz,
football for Geelong,
that I met my former teacher
in Celtic literature
at University College, Dublin,
though I've never been overseas in my life;
in my mind's eye, I've seen myself running,
pursued, afraid,
finally aware
that who was chasing me was me.

And I'm still running now.

Picture at an Exhibition: *Solo Man (homo softdrinkus)* c. 1975, Australia

Hairy-chested, moustachioed,
ruggedly handsome, tanned,
he lies naked on a lilo
in a backyard swimming pool,
eyes gazing at the camera,
an animal dumb half-smile,
sizeable snag,
sunlight glinting
off his blonde-haired scrotal sac
...but ladies, he'll find it absurd
to consider what you want,
sexually or otherwise.

Brief Biographical Sketch of Titian

Titian lived to be
an old bugger.
A painter-diplomat, he
was known to royalty
and many other notables of his day.
Unlike his fellow painters,
who were paid as humble artisans,
he became very rich;
so, when he was an old bugger,
he was also, at the same time,

an extremely lucky one.

This/That?

Lion and Rose?

Tiger and *Fleur-de-Lys*?

Headstone and Yew Tree?

Styx and Shangri-La?

A monster on a funeral pyre
floating in a sea of ice?

Chaos Theory

Someone in China sneezed
which caused me,
when watching the football on tele,
to drop my can of beer.

Variations on Some Lines from Plath's 'Lorelei'

O river I see drifting

O river I see – drifting –

drifting deep,

deep in your flux

deep in your flux

of silver,

silver

stone

stone

stone

stone

stone,

stone

ferry me

ferry me

down

down

down there.

The Geelong College Gates, Geelong, Victoria

There's a poem here, in these college gates
dedicated to an old boy
who lost his life while trying to save
another from drowning
in the waters off Ocean Grove
back in 1938.
There's definitely a poem in these gates
and for so long I've wanted to write it.
'Full fathom, full fathom, full fathom five...'
those words from *The Tempest* recur
as I struggle to find expression
for what I feel when I look at the gates
and read the plaque beside them:
'Greater love hath no man
than that he lay down his life...'
The scene is deeply moving
but, perhaps, after all,
my yearned-for poem
concerning the gates
in aptly-named Noble Street
has more to do with my romantic desire
to write about them,
than with the tragic event
that brought about their existence.

What I Remember About My Paternal Grandfather

He extolled the virtues of drinking beer
from glass as opposed to can

was fond of singing old songs
'All day, all night Mary-Ann' when drunk

would go duck shooting
then dump the unplucked birds
upon my suburban Mum's kitchen table
saying 'I've brought home dinner'

was a friendly bloke with family
but not a great mixer otherwise

a country yokel whom I loved.

When Colonel Sanders Met Colonel Tom Parker

When Colonel Sanders met Colonel Tom Parker,
the backslapping started, their laughing grew harder.

These entrepreneurs were two peas in a pod:
human caricatures, and equally odd.

Writer's Lament

I don't want to be shortlisted.
Let me drop without trace,
rather than hang on
by my fingernails.

I don't want to be shortlisted
– it's like being half-pregnant.

I don't want to be shortlisted.
The only thing worse
than being shortlisted
is the most awful thing in the world,

being longlisted.

All Hallows' Eve

Broody night.
Above a silent graveyard,
a crescent moon in a sky
pricked with lonely stars.
Headstones and monuments,
weathered, age-old,
spread into the distance.
Fumy mists swirl in the tombs,
rise to the air
become ghosts, link up,
ululate and dance
a hypnotic, circular ballet
– but soon they have vanished
back to grave-bound quietude.

Not Quite Yorick

I feel like Hamlet,
except that what I'm looking at
is not a skull.
The death mask I'm observing
is typical of such artefacts:
the subject appears dignified,
seems to have died content,
and displays a serene quality
that he rarely revealed in life.

When the Dead Return

When the dead return,
they're naked.
(No they're not,
but I knew saying that
would grab your attention.)

When the dead return...
they're boring.
Just stand at your bedside
when you're asleep,
or in corners of rooms,
or pin-drop off balconies
of tall buildings.

When the dead return,
they show
no imagination at all.

Semaphore, Adelaide

Something was haunting those humid, summery,
Semaphore streets
in 1980, when I was there,
aged eighteen,
visiting Iris, my grandmother,
with the rest of the family.
I walked the rain-spattered footpaths sensing
something.
I now realise it was *someone*
– *you*, Henry Reynolds,
great-great-grandfather,
who died in Semaphore's Blackler Street,
in March 1918,
though I didn't know it at the time.
Now, in 2020,
a question has finally formed in my head:
what were you trying to tell me,
forty years ago?
Probably nothing, except
that you were there,
watching me walk in your footsteps.

.   .   .

Henry, I can see you
tottering into your front garden,

jaundiced, asthenic,
touching a rose
a week before
the Spanish dancer swept you away
– the last time you left the house –
your beautiful wife, Janey,
watching from the verandah,
tears in her eyes,
which she didn't let you see.

To Die

There are many stories in which the condemned
walk to the gallows with courage,
meeting their death with dignity.
Not as often mentioned are those
who break down at the sight of the noose
– or firing squad, lethal injection, guillotine,
electric chair –
screaming for forgiveness.
Some tell lies *in extremis*, declaim,
blaming their capital crime on others.

Then there's the last woman hanged
in Victoria, Australia:
Jean Lee
– sedated, placed in a chair on the drop.
Was she unconscious beneath her hood,
as some suspect?
Or, simply, had no final words
before plunging to eternity?

www.ingramcontent.com/pod-product-compliance
Lightning Source LLC
Chambersburg PA
CBHW071919070526
44583CB00016B/2056